Another Second Poetry Book

compiled by John Foster

Oxford University Press

Oxford University Press, Great Clarendon Street, Oxford OX2 6DP

Oxford   New York
Athens   Auckland   Bangkok   Bogota   Buenos Aires   Calcutta
Cape Town   Chennai   Dar es Salaam   Delhi   Florence
Hong Kong   Istanbul   Karachi   Kuala Lumpur   Madrid
Melbourne   Mexico City   Mumbai   Nairobi   Paris   São Paulo
Singapore   Taipei   Tokyo   Toronto   Warsaw

and associated companies in
Berlin   Ibadan

Oxford is a trade mark of Oxford University Press

First published in paperback 1988
Reprinted 1989, 1993, 1995, 1997, 1998

A CIP record for this book is available from the British Library

ISBN 0 19 918229 8

Phototypeset by Tradespools Limited, Frome, Somerset
Printed in Hong Kong

Contents

The Secret Song

Who saw the petals
   drop from the rose?
I, said the spider,
But nobody knows.

Who saw the sunset
   flash on a bird?
I, said the fish,
But nobody heard.

Who saw the fog
   come over the sea?
I, said the sea pigeon,
Only me.

Who saw the first
   green light of the sun?
I, said the night owl,
The only one.

Who saw the moss
   creep over the stone?
I, said the gray fox,
All alone.

Margaret Wise Brown

Our Pond

The pond in our garden
Is murky and deep
And lots of things live there
That slither and creep,

Like diving bell spiders
And great ramshorn snails
And whirligig beetles
And black snappertails.

There used to be goldfish
That nibbled my thumb,
But now there's just algae
And sour, crusty scum.

There used to be pondweed
With fizzy green shoots,
But now there are leeches
And horrible newts.

One day when my football
Rolled in by mistake
I tried to retrieve it
By using a rake,

But as I leaned over
A shape from the ooze
Bulged up like a nightmare
And lunged at my shoes.

I ran back in shouting,
But everyone laughed
And said I was teasing
Or else I was daft.

But I know what happened
And when I'm asleep
I dream of those creatures
That slither and creep:

The diving bell spiders
And great ramshorn snails
And whirligig beetles
And black snappertails.

Richard Edwards

The Tree in Season

Spring
The tree hums quietly to itself
a lullaby to the buds
bursting with baby leaves
its branches ride the winds
and in all its new green glory
the tree begins to sing

Summer
The tree stretches in the sun
it knows the birds that fly
the beasts that run, climb and jump
from its heavy loaded branches
it yawns and digs its roots
deep into the still centre
of the spinning earth

Autumn
The tree shivers in the shortening day
its leaves turn gold
the clouds pass
the seeds fall
the tree drops its coins of gold
and the days are rich
with the spending of leaves

Winter
Old branches ache
the tree stands naked in the storms
frozen bleak and bare
deep underground life lies sleeping
the tree sleeps
and waits for the returning sun
to wake him
from his woody dreams

Robert Fisher

11

Winter

Winter crept
through the whispering wood,
hushing fir and oak;
crushed each leaf and froze each web –
but never a word he spoke.

Winter prowled
by the shivering sea,
lifting sand and stone;
nipped each limpet silently –
and then moved on.

Winter raced
down the frozen stream,
catching at his breath;
on his lips were icicles,
at his back was death.

Judith Nicholls

Change

I didn't see one fall,
Not a single leaf at all
From the tree beyond the wall.
And now it's bare
With winter
Almost there.

Although I was awake
I didn't see one flake
Fall to the frozen lake.
And now it's white
Within one
Wintered night.

I thought I might have seen
A nudging shoot of green
Oh, where could I have been?
And now birds sing
The season's clean:
Another spring.

John Kitching

14

Snow

I've just woken up and I'm lying in bed
With the end of a dream going round in my head,
And something much quieter and softer than rain
Is brushing the window pane.

It's snowing! It's snowing! My room's filled with light.
Outside it's like Switzerland, eveything's white.
That bulge is our dustbin, that hummock's the wall.
I can't see the flower-beds at all.

I've got to get out there. I've got to get dressed.
I can't find my pants and I can't find my vest.
Who's taken my jumper? Who's hidden my belt?
It might be beginning to melt!

I'm outside, I'm running. I'm up to my waist.
I'm rolling. I'm tasting the metally taste.
There's snow down my trousers and snow up my nose.
I can't even feel my toes.

I'm tracking a polar bear over the ice,
I'm making a snow-man, he's fallen down twice,
I'm cutting some steps to the top of the hedge,
Tomorrow I'm building a sledge.

I'm lying in bed again, tucked up tight;
I know I'll sleep soundly and safely tonight.
My snow-man's on guard and his shiny black eyes
Are keeping a look-out for spies.

Sleep quietly, sleep deeply, sleep calmly, sleep curled
In warm woolly blankets while out in the world,
On field and forest and mountain and town
The snow flakes like feathers float down.

Richard Edwards

The Frozen Man

Out at the edge of town
where black trees
crack their fingers
in the icy wind
and hedges freeze
on their shadows
and the breath of cattle,
still as boulders,
hangs in rags
under the rolling moon,
a man is walking
alone:

on the coal-black road
his cold
    feet
    ring
        and
        ring.
Here in a snug house
at the heart of town
the fire is burning
red and yellow and gold:
    you can hear the warmth
    like a sleeping cat
            breathe softly
            in every room.
When the frozen man
comes to the door,

let him in,
let him in,
let him in.

Kit Wright

16

Our Goalie

A raggy pair of gloves for hands,
our snowman stands in the goal.
His eyes are bright green bottle glass,
his teeth are bits of coal.

He has a carrot for a nose
from which an icicle drips.
The buttons down his front are stones,
his ears are my bicycle clips.

His nose and ears are battered,
and he's lost his big black smile,
so when we shoot the ball, we try
to miss him by a mile.

He does his best to keep the goal
as we practise taking shots,
but every time he stops a ball
some part of him drops off.

Next day, I go back on my bike
to see if he still stands.
– But all that's left is a drift of snow
and the empty gloves of his hands.

James Kirkup

Snowy Morning

Wake
gently this morning
to a different day.
Listen.

There is no bray
of buses,
no brake growls,
no siren howls and
no horns
blow.
There is only
the silence
of a city
hushed
by snow.

Lilian Moore

My Sledge

As I drag it
over crusty snow
it follows me –
a dog at heel –
sometimes catching
up with me, now
at left, now at right,
sniffing my snowboots
with a soft bang
of its metal noses,
tip-tilted runners
shining-wet
that slither-slide
from side to side –

till they jerk back
at a bare patch, where
old snow has melted,
and there, like ponies
scenting bad water
or unseen dangers,
dig in their heels
and obstinately refuse
to move on to
the next good patch of snow,
where I can toboggan
from this hilltop height
into the soft snowdrifts
of meadows far below.

So I carry them over, and then
we are back in our element again.

James Kirkup

Playground Count

One on a bench
Sitting alone
Knees up to chin
Hair needing a comb.

Two by the fence
In a tight gossip huddle.

Three on the ground
All in a muddle
Kicking and yelling not heeding the puddle.

Four with a skipping rope
Chanting and counting,

Five in a queue by the water fountain,

Six by the gate, five jeering one pouting,

Seven with a football stuck on the roof
Which they can't get down by shouting.

Eight singing disco
In a row on the wall,

Nine with a bag of crisps,
Not enough for all.

Forty five children line up forty two
Minus –
One graze and one nose bleed
And one who's wet through.

Now the playground is free
For ten sparrows to see
What's left in the crisp bag
Thrown under the tree.

Julie Holder

School break

throwing grass
handstands

running
chasing
laugh

pass the ball
daisychains
tag me as you pass

sunshine
rain-pool splashing

hop
with arms
spread wide

smell of hawthorn
blossom

best friend
by my side

lie down
sunray spreading

wind on face
in hair

short time
warm time
fun share

joke
and cry
and care

Joan Poulson

Shirley Said

Who wrote 'kick me' on my back?
Who put a spider in my mack?
Who's the one who pulls my hair?
Tries to trip me everywhere?
Who runs up to me and strikes me?
That boy there – I think he likes me.

Dennis Doyle

23

Infant School Disaster

Peter pushed past Pauline
and Pauline pushed past Paul
so Peter pushed Paul sideways
then Pauline pushed them all....
Peter knocked the fire bell
and Pauline gave a shout
the dinner ladies heard them
and they all came running out!
They overturned their custard
and they slipped upon their sprouts
and upset all their puddings
and they upset all their stew.....
The shepherds pie went flying
the pig bins went as well...
...then Pauline pushed past Peter
        and tried to stop the bell.
The teachers all came running
they met a sea of stew
and slipped in all the jelly
(the way that people do)
The teachers all went sprawling
in custard chips and peas
– jelly on their jackets
– and gravy on their knees.

Peter Dixon

Windows

On the way to my classroom
I walk down the long corridor,
past the hundreds of books,
their picture jackets
colourful and bright,
each one a window onto worlds
I have never visited.

I can see elephants
on a plain in Africa,
a jet airliner cruising
far above the white clouds,
waterfalls, icebergs,
and cavemen fighting a sabre-tooth
while the family cowers in a cave.

Such places! Such worlds!
Back in class there are windows
looking onto a world I know well.
I see the deserted playground,
the grey, November sky,
rows of houses and beyond these
the chimney of a closed-down factory.

I'm always willing
to take the register to the Office,
or messages to other classrooms
for then I can walk down
the long corridor and gaze once more
through the book jacket windows
onto worlds I have never visited.

Wes Magee

I Went Back

I went back after a cold
And nothing was the same.
When the register was called
Even my name
Sounded queer...new...
(And I was born here too!)
Everyone knew more than me,
Even Kenneth Hannaky
Who's worst usually.
They'd made a play
And puppets from clay
While I was away,
Learnt a song about Cape Horn,
Five guinea pigs were born.
Daffodils in the blue pot,
(I planted them)
Bloomed, and I was not
There to see.
Jean had a new coat
And someone, probably George,
Smashed my paper boat.
Monday was a dreadful day.
I wished I was still away.
Tuesday's news day.
I took my stamps to show,
Made a clown called Jo,
Learnt that song from John...
Cold's almost gone...
And...the smallest guinea pig,
Silky black and brown thing,
I'm having
Till spring.

Gwen Dunn

Change of Mind

In first lesson Johnny,
Johnny not so bright
Swapped his pen for an answer
Which then he couldn't write.

In the playground Johnny,
Johnny lack a day,
Swapped his boots
For a football with a puncture
That he couldn't kick anyway.

At lunchtime Johnny,
Johnny just his luck
Swapped his small bag
For a big bag
Full of crumbs for the duck.

At hometime Johnny,
Johnny where's your cap again?
Fed the ducks as he cried unseen tears
Swapping them with the rain.

Somewhere on the way home Johnny,
Johnny on the train
Swapped himself for another boy
And was never the same again.

Julie Holder

29

How to Get There

I go
through Sunday's tunnel, hushed and deep;
up Monday's mountain, craggy and steep;
along Tuesday's trail, winding and slow;
into Wednesday's woods, still halfway to go;
over Thursday's bridge, shaky and tall;
through the hidden gate in Friday's wall
to get to
SATURDAY.

I wish there were a shorter way.

Bonnie Nims

The Tunnel

The lights go on in the mainline diesel
And sounding its horn like a challenge
At the dark entrance of the tunnel
It threads it like a needle.

A train of reflected shadows and light
Charges beside us on the wall,
Into the tunnel, under the hill,
Through half-a-mile of night.

The train's swift-moving shining thread
Fastens the sunshine
It has left behind
To the sunshine ahead.

Stanley Cook

Saturday

What's Saturday, mate?
Saturday's GREAT!
It's stay-up-late.

Saturday's
Natterday,
Eat-and-grow-fatter-day.

Saturday's
Clatter-day,
Chip chop and chatter day.

Saturday's
Scatter-day,

Never get up
Cos it don't really matter-day.

It's a that-a-day,
SATURDAY.

Anon.

Month by Month

Jan you really are cold.
Feb you're even colder.
March with a spring in your step.
April has a smile on her face.
Maybe the sun will shine, maybe it won't.
D'you know it's meant to be summer.
D'you lie getting a suntan,
Or gusts of spray in your face?
Sept-ember's glowing red cheeks.
Octo-burns the autumn leaves.
N-N-November's chillness.
Dis ember is flickering... stillness.

John Foster

Weak Week

Monday – not much of a fun-day
Tuesday – hometown blues day
Wednesday – same againsday
Thursday – bit of a blursday
Friday – didn't want to tryday
Saturday – an even flatter day
Sunday – stale bunday

John Kitching

Wellie Weather

Steamed-up rainy pane days
Twirling weather-vane days
Red-hot fingered chilblain days –
                    Wellie weather

Icy underfoot days
Snow transformed to soot days
All mothers' scold and tut days –
                    Wellie weather.

Shivering stray cat days
'Don't forget your hat!' days
Nice children turned to brats days –
                    Wellie weather.

Half the class away days
Games-field turned to clay days
Indoor dinner-time play days –
                    Wellie weather.

Gas-fire turned up to three days
Scalding-hot soup for tea days
Watching far too much T.V. days –
                    Wellie weather!

Jacqueline Brown

Wet Winter Evening

Dinners are cooking
All down the street.
Pans bubble
To radios' voices and beat.
Steam on the window,
Rain on the glass,
Dogs barking as home going footsteps pass.

The birds that beaded branches
Have flown.
The stars are seeded
But not grown
'Till the eye of the moon
Through curtains of cloud
Looks down to greet,
Lamplight blossoms, heads bowed
In the desert of street.

The trees stand pewter and ebony,
The pavement shines silver and jet.
Inside T.V.s are turned on,
Plates clatter
And tables are set.

Children rub steam
From the windows
To stare into the mist of the rain.
They sigh for something to happen
And wish for the summer again.

Later, curled warm in their beds,
Hot water bottle suns at their feet,
They sleep to the sigh of the wind
And the gurgle of rain in the street.

Julie Holder

35

Storm

They're at it again
the wind and the rain
It all started
when the wind
took the window
by the collar
and shook it
with all its might
Then the rain
butted in
What a din
they'll be at it all night
Serves them right
if they go home in the morning
and the sky won't let them in

Roger McGough

Monsoon

Where do the fish go
When the monsoon
Thunders on the water
And the foam churns
Like milk?

Where do the birds hide
When the trees fall
In high winds
And all the fruit
Lies everywhere
On field and ground?

Where do people run
When the rain comes through
The thatch,
And the floods creep in on them
Like thieves?

Alfreda de Silva

Hurricane

Under low black clouds
the wind was all
speedy feet, all horns and breath,
all bangs, howls, rattles,
in every hen house,
church hall and school.

Roaring, screaming, returning,
it made forced entry, shoved walls,
made rifts, brought roofs down,
hitting rooms to sticks apart.

It wrung soft banana trees,
broke tough trunks of palms.
It pounded vines of yams,
left fields battered up.

Invisible with such ecstasy—
with no intervention of sun or man—
everywhere kept changing branches.

Zinc sheets are kites.
Leaves are panic swarms.
Fowls are fixed with feathers turned.
Goats, dogs, pigs,
all are people together.

Then growling it slunk away
from muddy, mossy trail and boats
in hedges: and cows, ratbats, trees,
fish, all dead in the road.

James Berry

The Storm

(A Poem to use as a play)

There is a snuffling round the door
The sandgrains scatter on the cave floor,
There is a howling in the trees
It's the wolf ghost wind that leaves no spoor.

The wolf breath is in their mouths and round their
ears.
And Grandmother pushes the door stone tighter
She seems not afraid the wolf ghost will bite her.

There is a flickering in the air
Through the smoke hole we see clouds torn,
There is a flash that splits the sky
It's the dancing blade of the storm.

The blade is in their hands and in their hearts.

And Grandmother builds the fire brighter
She seems not afraid the blade will strike her.

There is a rattling of spears in the river
There is a fast and faster drumming,
The spring in the cave brims the well
The rain god is coming.

The beat is in their blood. Fire smoke blurs their eyes.

And Grandmother bids us as her mother taught her
To salute with cupped hands the fall of water.

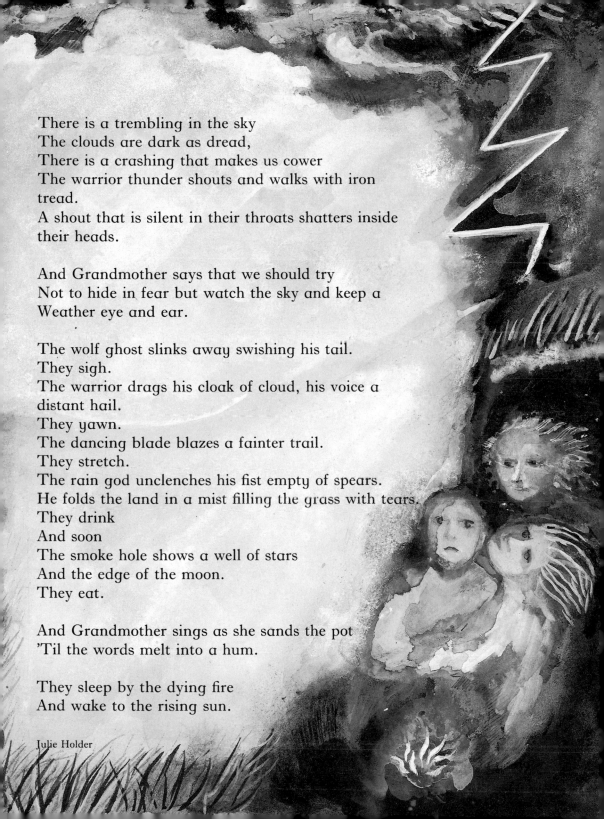

There is a trembling in the sky
The clouds are dark as dread,
There is a crashing that makes us cower
The warrior thunder shouts and walks with iron
tread.
A shout that is silent in their throats shatters inside
their heads.

And Grandmother says that we should try
Not to hide in fear but watch the sky and keep a
Weather eye and ear.

The wolf ghost slinks away swishing his tail.
They sigh.
The warrior drags his cloak of cloud, his voice a
distant hail.
They yawn.
The dancing blade blazes a fainter trail.
They stretch.
The rain god unclenches his fist empty of spears.
He folds the land in a mist filling the grass with tears.
They drink
And soon
The smoke hole shows a well of stars
And the edge of the moon.
They eat.

And Grandmother sings as she sands the pot
'Til the words melt into a hum.

They sleep by the dying fire
And wake to the rising sun.

Julie Holder

Take Two

A bruise of wind
fists the street;
a knuckle of rain
punches south.

The shutters bark
back and the moon
coughs discreetly.

Night nibbles the dawn.

The stars lose control.

Pie Corbett

Thunder in the Mountains

Clenched fists of grim clouds,
tense knuckles whitened, waiting
for the first forked flash.

James Kirkup

40

The Wind in a Tree

The wind in a tree,
Makes a sound like the sea.

The branches toss like breakers;
...green horses.

John Cunliffe

Count me out

It's not that
I'm a scaredy cat,
it's just that
I don't like caves,
and the feeling of doom
in the colourless gloom
flowing over you
in waves.

It's the way
your voice rolls
round and around,
echoing low and weird,
and your torch becomes
such a little light,
each shadow one
to be feared.

It's the way
the clammy cold
grips you, chills you
through to your very bones,
and how every sound
when you're underground
is some unspeakable thing
that groans.

It's the way
that you slip
on slime underfoot and it's
hard to remember the sun,
so when kids want to explore
all the caves on the shore
I say, 'Count me out.
It's no fun!'

Moira Andrew

The Lighthouse

THIS IS THE LIGHTHOUSE BUILT OF STONE
Erected by Sir William Bone;

This is the lamp that shone in the tower
That Bone built.

This is the oil
That filled the lamp
That shone in the tower
That Bone built.

This is the barrel
That carried the oil
That filled the lamp
That shone in the tower
That Bone built.

This is the boat
That brought the barrel
That carried the oil
That filled the lamp
That shone in the tower
That Bone built.

43

This is the man
Who rowed the boat
That brought the barrel
That carried the oil
That filled the lamp
That shone in the tower
That Bone built.

This is the woman
Who married the man
Who rowed the boat
That brought the barrel
That carried the oil
That filled the lamp
That shone in the tower
That Bone built.

This is the daughter
Who lived with the woman
Who married the man
Who rowed the boat
That brought the barrel
That carried the oil
That filled the lamp
That shone in the tower
That Bone built.

This is the bedroom
Of the girl
Who lived with the woman
Who married the man
Who rowed the boat
That brought the barrel
That carried the oil
That filled the lamp
That shone in the tower
That Bone built.

This is the window
Of the room
Where the lonely girl
Who lived with the woman
Who married the man
Who rowed the boat
That brought the barrel
That carried the oil
That filled the lamp
That shone in the tower
That Bone built
Can stand and gaze at the lantern rail
Where the sea-gulls swoop and squawk and wail
Around the head of the lighthouse man
Who keeps the lamp
That burns the oil
That's poured from the barrel
That's brought by the boat
That's rowed by the man
Who married the woman
Who lived with the girl
Who stands by the pane
And again and again
Waves through the sunshine and the rain
At the keeper on the tower of stone
Erected by Sir Willian Bone.

Gregory Harrison

The Sand Castle

Out of the fresh, damp sand
well below the seaweed line,
we start to dig, and build a fine
sand castle shadowed by the cliffs.

It's the biggest sand castle ever built.
We give it moats and turrets,
flights of steps, a drawbridge made
from the lid of a pencil box.

It has many a window of shining shell,
dungeons and gateways, courtyards too
all paved and arched with wave-worn stones.
There's a clock that never tells the time.

And on the topmost tower, we plant
a flagpole, with a purple flag
of silver paper from a chocolate bar,
to show we're in residence, like royalty.

The low tide begins to turn. We have to move
closer and closer to the promenade
before the battle of the breakers,
the distant thunder of the surf's big guns.

We watch the first wave fill the moat.
The next ones swamp the drawbridge, then
the gateway to the courtyard crumbles.
The clock now will never tell the time.

Still our flag flies bravely on!
We're holding out against the foe!
But even that proud tower falls in ruins,
and the flag sinks in the swell.

As we pack our things to go back home
we take a last long look. Our castle's gone.
It's a castle far below the waves,
where the Sea King's in residence now.

James Kirkup

Floating a Plate

I like doing the washing up,
Squirting green liquid
into the bottom of our red bowl;
watching it sud and foam
like cream soda,
feeling the froth,
as I launch saucers as submarines
cups and pans as diving bells,
in a sea where knives are sharks
and forks become spiny sea-urchins,
while dunked glasses
surface as smiling and hopeful jellyfish
that slip through the wrinkle and pucker of my
fingers.
Most of all though I like washing plates
so I keep them back until last of all.
When the bubbles have all gone and grease floats
on the surface like an oil slick,
carefully I float the plates across a Sargasso Sea
of spaghetti strands and soggy lettuce leaves,
watching as they slowly sink one after the other
like so many pale moons beneath the water;
when the last one has gone
washing up ceases to be fun.

Frank Flynn

49

The Itch

If your hands get wet
in the washing-up water,
if they get covered in flour,
if you get grease or oil
all over your fingers,
if they land up in the mud,
wet grit, paint, or glue...

have you noticed
it's just then
that you always get
a terrible itch
just inside your nose?
And you can try to
twitch your nose,
twist your nose,
squeeze your nose,
scratch it with your arm,
scrape your nose on
your shoulder
or press it
up against the wall,
but it's no good.
You can't get rid of
the itch.
It drives you so mad
you just have to let a
finger get at it.
And before you know
you've done it.
you've wiped a load of glue,
or oil,
or cold wet pastry
all over the end of your nose.

Michael Rosen

Kitchen Adventure

Out of matchsticks
He created a temple.

Out of cabbage-leaves
A child lost in the jungle.
The beetle became a jackal.
Hyena laughter covered his kitchen table like spilt
soup.

The boy, who called him grandad,
Obliged him by shrinking in size
To a couple of millimetres tall.
Some hours –
And a great many helicopter-whirrings by the boy's
mother – later
They were found by the search party,
Crossing the butter-dish glacier,
Luckily, both uninjured.

Leo Aylen

51

The Useful Art of Knitting

When Mum sits down to knit at night
Her patterns seem to go just right.
She doesn't even have to look;
She can knit and read a book.
But, oh, the worry
And the flurry
When I sit
And try to knit!
My stitches always get too tight
Or else I drop them out of sight.
I split the wool and big holes come,
I pass my knitting back to Mum.
I grizzle and I grumble,
I struggle and I mumble.
I feel just like that girl Matilda
('The effort very nearly killed her.')
Mum says, 'Don't worry, try once more.'
I throw my knitting on the floor.
We both get cross; I go to bed
And a wonderful dream comes into my head:
When my knitting is finished
I shall win First Prize
for
The Most Original
Best Ventilated
Multi-coloured
Complicated
Scarf
Knitted by a Demented Spider
For an Oddly-shaped Snake
With a Very
Sore Throat.

Katherine Craig

Knitting

She tried to knit a night-cap,
She tried to knit a scarf,
She tried to knit a cardigan,
Too big they were, by half.

She tried to knit a waistcoat,
She tried to knit a shawl,
She tried to knit a bobble hat,
But they turned out too small.

And now she's knitting knickers,
And if *they* do not fit,
We'll make her wear them anyhow,
Until she's learned to knit.

Colin West

53

The Friday Night Smell

I love the
friday night
smell of
mammie baking
bread ———— creeping
up to me in
bed, and tho
zzzz I'll fall
asleep, before i
even get a
bite —— when
morning come,
you can bet
I'll meet a
kitchen table
laden with
bread, still
warm and fresh
salt bread
sweet bread
crisp and brown
& best of all
coconut buns
THAT's why
I love the
friday night
smell of mammie
baking bread
putting me to
sleep, dreaming
of jumping from
the highest branch
of the jamoon tree
into the red water
creek

beating calton
run & catching
the biggest fish
in the world
plus, getting
the answers right
to every single
sum
that every day
in my dream
begins and ends
with the friday
night smell of
mammie baking
bread, and
coconut buns
of course.

Marc Matthews

I'm Alone in the Evening

I'm alone in the evening
when the family sits
reading and sleeping
and I watch the fire in close
to see flame goblins
wriggling out of their caves
for the evening

Later I'm alone
when the bath has gone cold around me
and I have put my foot
beneath the cold tap
where it can dribble
through valleys between my toes
out across the white plain of my foot
and bibble bibble into the sea

I'm alone
when mum's switched out the light
my head against the pillow
listening to ca thump ca thump
in the middle of my ears.
It's my heart.

Michael Rosen

Bedtime

the day is over
the night comes gently
the bathtub water
                       is green and warm
the little girl comes down the stairs
gaily
shining from her bath
like a Christmas ball

the fire dances for her
like a princess swaying swaying

and her mother when she kisses her goodnight
is soft
with pillow smell

she hears the wind ruffling outside
saying sleep sleep sleep

Charlotte Zolotow

57

After Dark

What is it like
after dark
in the park ?
I mean to find out if I can.
Does the tiger whose lair's
in the laurel bush there
come out for a prowl
when he hears the night owl
after dark
in the park ?

Or do all the children
tucked up in their beds
come in their dreams to play,
and invisibly swing on the swings in the night
after dark
in the park ?

Sheila Simmons

58

I Like to Stay Up

I like to stay up
and listen
when big people talking
jumbie stories

Oooooooooooooooooooh
I does feel so tingly
and excited
inside – eeeeeeeeeeee

But when my mother say
'Girl, time for bed'
then is when
I does feel a dread
then is when
I does jump into me bed
then is when
I does cover up
from me feet to me head

then is when
I does wish
I didn't listen
to no stupid jumbie story
then is when
I does wish
I did read me book instead

Grace Nichols

When Dracula Went to the Blood Bank

When Dracula went to the blood bank,
he thoroughly flustered the staff,
for rather than make a donation,
he drew out a pint and a half.

Jack Prelutsky

60

Vampire Visit

A pint of blood is all I need
To get me through the night,
A tiny peck around the neck
Will fill me with delight.

I'm sure you have a pint to spare,
Your veins look fairly ample,
So, save a vampire from despair
And let me have a sample.

Please put away that wooden stake,
It looks a trifle sharp.
Be careful now, for heaven's sake,
You'll stab me through the hea-a-a-a-a-a-a-a-rt

Doug Macleod

61

Hob-goblin

I am nothing-man
Dwelling in dark
Gobbling blackness into my guts
I am nothing-man
Choking in smoke
Chewing the sooty bits round in my lungs
I am hot-foot, coal-hopper, nip.
I stir the night's ashes up with my heels
I am red-eyes, brittle-blazing
Cracking sparks at my finger-ends.
All life long I hear the spittle-purr of flames
And I crackle back my love to their leaping hearts.

Berlie Doherty

In Black Chasms

In black chasms, in caves where water
Drops and drips, in pits deep under the ground,
The ogres wait. A thousand years will not
Alter them. They are hideous, bad-tempered,
Bound only to be cruel, enemies of all.
Slow-moving, lazy, their long hard arms
Are strong as bulldozers, their red eyes
Gleam with deceit. When they smile,
It is not with kindness. In their language
They have no words for friendship, honesty,
Loyalty, generosity. Their names are
Bully, Slyness, Greed, Vandal and Cunning.
They hate light, and quarrel among themselves.
A single ogre will pass by, or only threaten
In his loud, rough voice, but they are dangerous
In packs. Be on your guard against them, keep
Always a brave front, value your friends,
For they are needed against ogres.

Leslie Norris

63

Midnight Forest

Who wanders wild
in moon and puffball light
where night sleeps black
and spiders creep?
What is that sound
that stills the air?
Whose is the breath
that rustles oak and fir?
Beware,
the tree-gods stir.

Judith Nicholls

Timeless

There is no clock in the forest
but a dandelion to blow,
an owl that hunts
when the light has gone,
a mouse that sleeps
till night has come,
lost in the moss below.

There is no clock in the forest,
only the cuckoo's song
and the thin white
of the early dawn,
the pale damp-bright
of a waking June,
the bluebell light
of a day half-born
when the stars have gone.

There is no clock in the forest.

Judith Nicholls

Don't Panic

That beating at my bedroom pane:
It's only wind and driving rain.
Relax.

That awful blind and blurry mass:
Nothing but rain streaks on the glass.
Harmless.

That monstrous shadow leaning in,
Wearing an evil twisted grin:
It's just the ivy plant that's all
Bobbing and tossing on the wall.
Don't panic.

That scratching from my bedroom floor:
It's just a mouse, he's been before.
No sweat.

That rustling – is it just the draught?
Or giant spiders? Don't be daft!
Couldn't be.

The loops this new wallpaper makes:
Just loops, not coiled and deadly snakes.
Absurd!

Suppose there are though – snakes, I mean,
And evil spirits sidling in,
And ghosts and blobs and phantom riders
And armies of advancing spiders,
And vampires stalking through the gloom,
All closing in upon my room...

HELP!

Eric Finney

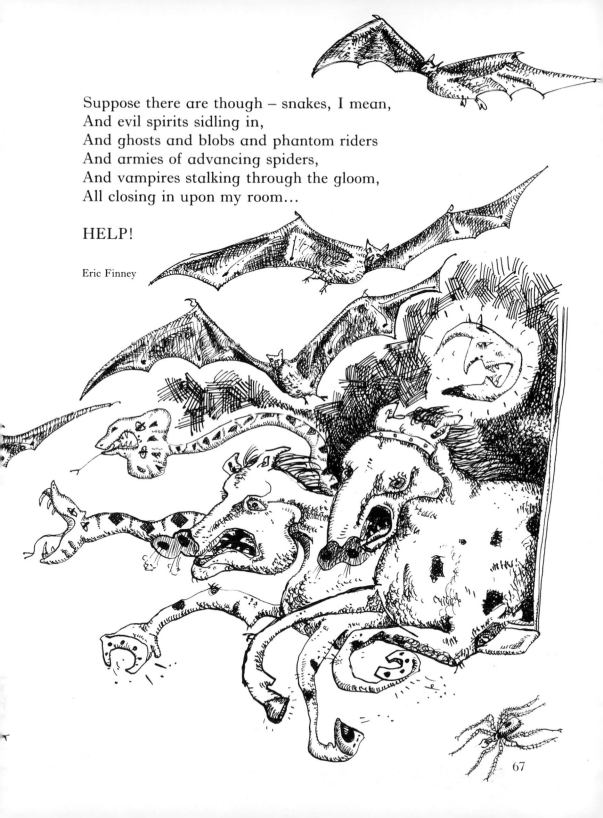

Early to Bed

The thing I can't stand
About grown-ups
Is the way
They say
You can't stay up late
To watch TV.
They make you
Go off to bed
Then keep you awake
By watching themselves
Till it closes down,
While you're lying in bed
With the noise
Of the programmes
Drumming through your head.

Then, in the morning,
When you're yawning,
And they're being crabby
Because they're tired
From staying up too late,
They say:
There you are, you see,
You stayed up too late
Watching TV.
It's early to bed
For you tonight.
And they rush off to work
Thinking they're right.

John Foster

Tricks

Nearly every morning
my brother would lie in bed,
lift his hands up in the air
full stretch
then close his hands around an invisible bar.
'Ah, my magic bar,' he'd say.
Then he'd heave on the bar,
pull himself up,
until he was sitting up in bed.

Then he'd get up.
I said,
'You haven't got a magic bar above your bed.'
'I have,' he said.
'You haven't,' I said.
'Don't believe me then,' he said.
'I won't – don't worry,' I said.
'It doesn't make any difference to me
if you do or you don't,' he said,
and went out of the room.

'Magic bar!' I said.
'Mad. He hasn't got a magic bar.'
I made sure he'd gone downstairs,
then I walked over to his bed
and waved my hand about in the air
above his pillow.
'I knew it,' I said to myself.
'Didn't fool me for a moment.'

Michael Rosen

Huff

I am in a tremendous huff –
Really, really bad.
It isn't any ordinary huff –
It's one of the best I've had.

I plan to keep it up for a month
Or maybe for a year
And you needn't think you can make me smile
Or talk to you. No fear.

I can do without you and her and them –
Too late to make amends.
I'll think deep thoughts on my own for a while,
Then find some better friends.

And they'll be wise and kind and good
And bright enough to see
That they should behave with proper respect
Towards somebody like me.

I do love being in a huff –
Cold fury is so heady.
I've been like this for half an hour
And I feel better already.

Perhaps I'll give them another chance,
Now I'm feeling stronger,
But they'd better watch out – my next big huff
Could last much, much, much longer.

Wendy Cope

70

Grudges

It isn't fair …
that I must be in bed
for hours before,
that I get all the blame
and never her,
that she's allowed to choose
what she will wear,
it isn't fair!

It isn't right …
that she's allowed out
late at night,
that she can *choose* when to
switch off her light,
that *I'm* the one told off
whenever there's a fight,
it isn't right!

It makes me mad …
that they think she's so good
and I'm so bad,
that she gets extra cash
for helping dad,
that *her* old coats are all
I've ever had,
it makes me mad!

*(I know I'm nine
and she is seventeen;
that's no excuse at all
for them to be so MEAN!)*

Judith Nicholls

71

Do You Mind?

Do you mind, my mum says,
Not squeezing the toothpaste tube
In the middle and leaving it
A shapeless squashy mess;
And do you mind
Not just fishing the strawberries
Out of the strawberry jam
But eating some of the jelly stuff
In between as well;
And another thing:
Do you mind putting your
Toenail clippings in the waste bin
Instead of shooting them
All round the bathroom;
And my dad joins in with
Oh yes, and while we're about it
Do you mind
Not filling the car's ashtrays
With sticky sweet papers
So that I get goo on my fingers
Every time I put out a fag;
And my sister,
Who's enjoying this, says
Do you mind leaving my comb alone:
I'm forever cleaning your
Ratty old hairs out of it.

Well actually, I *do* mind
And I'm thinking of a few things
To throw back at
You perfect people.
But for now:
Do you mind packing in the
Nagging, niggling, binding, bitching,
Picking, pecking and criticizing and
Do you mind getting off my back and
Do you mind me screaming
HELP!

Eric Finney

HELP!

'Who the cap fit, let dem wear it'

If it wasn't you
who tek de chalk
and mark up de wall
juggle with de egg
and mek it fall
then why you didn't answer
when you hear Granny call?

If it wasn't you
who bounce yuh ball
in de goldfish bowl
wipe mud from yuh shoes
all over de floor
and poke yuh finger
straight in de butter

If it wasn't you
then why yuh heart a-flutter?
why yuh voice a-stutter?
and why you look so jumpy
when you stand up in front of Granny?

'Who the cap fit,
let dem wear it.'
That's what Granny does always say
and that she wasn't born yesterday.

John Agard

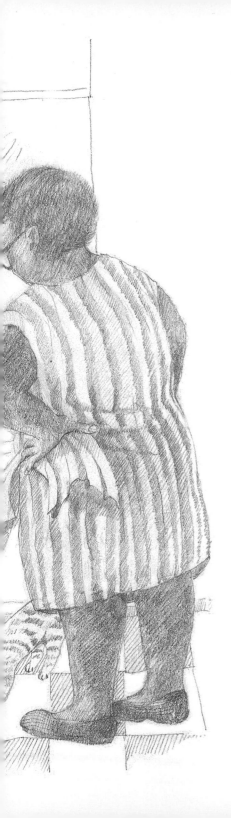

Beware

If you don't want a voice
With a bull-frog croak,
Take my advice:
Don't start to smoke.

If you don't want breath
Like a dirty joke,
Take my advice:
Don't start to smoke

If you don't want lungs
Filled with sooty coke,
Take my advice:
Don't start to smoke.

If you don't want a heart
Renewing one you broke,
Take my advice:
Don't start to smoke.

John Kitching

My Mother Says I'm Sickening

My mother says I'm sickening,
my mother says I'm crude,
she says this when she sees me
playing Ping-Pong with my food,
she doesn't seem to like it
when I slurp my bowl of stew,
and now she's got a list of things
she says I mustn't do—

DO NOT CATAPULT THE CARROTS!
DO NOT JUGGLE GOBS OF FAT!
DO NOT DROP THE MASHED POTATOES
ON THE GERBIL OR THE CAT!
NEVER PUNCH THE PUMPKIN PUDDING!
NEVER TUNNEL THROUGH THE BREAD!
PUT NO PEAS INTO YOUR POCKET!
PLACE NO NOODLES ON YOUR HEAD!
DO NOT SQUEEZE THE STEAMED ZUCCHINI!
DO NOT MAKE THE MELON OOZE!
NEVER STUFF VANILLA YOGURT
IN YOUR LITTLE SISTER'S SHOES!
DRAW NO FACES IN THE KETCHUP!
MAKE NO LITTLE GRAVY POOLS!

I wish my mother wouldn't make
so many useless rules.

Jack Prelutsky

Chicken Dinner

Mama, don' do it, please,
Don' cook dat chicken fe dinner,
We know dat chicken from she hatch,
She is de only one in de batch
Dat de mangoose didn' catch,
Don' bother cook her fe dinner.

'Mama, don' do it, please,
Don' cook dat chicken fe dinner,
Yuh mean to tell mi yuh feget
Yuh promise her to we as a pet
She not even have a chance to lay yet
An yuh going to cook her fe dinner.

Mama, don' do it, please,
Don' cook dat chicken fe dinner,
Don' give Henrietta de chop,
Ah tell yuh what, we could swop,
We could get yuh another one from de shop,
If yuh promise not to cook her fe dinner.

Mama, me really glad, yuh know,
Yuh never cook Henny fe dinner,
An she glad too, ah bet,
Oh gosh, me suddenly feel upset,
Yuh don' suppose is somebody pet
We eating now fe dinner?

Valerie Bloom

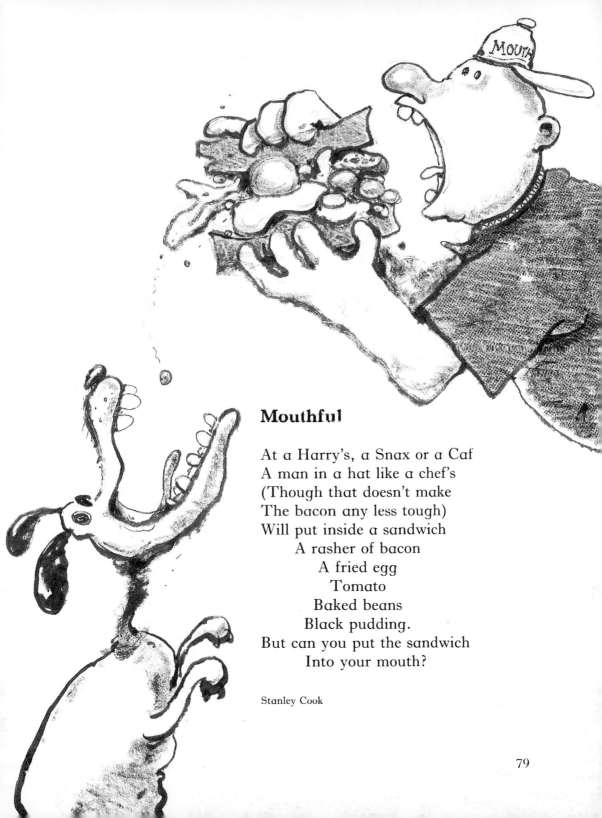

Mouthful

At a Harry's, a Snax or a Caf
A man in a hat like a chef's
(Though that doesn't make
The bacon any less tough)
Will put inside a sandwich
    A rasher of bacon
      A fried egg
       Tomato
     Baked beans
     Black pudding.
But can you put the sandwich
    Into your mouth?

Stanley Cook

79

Visit to de Dentist

Wat a likkle cry baby!
Look ow de bwoy a bawl,
One likkle injection im get
Im no ha no shame at all.

Ah bet im older dan mi, Mama,
But mi wouldn' cry so loud,
In fac' mi wouldn' cry at all
Especially eena crowd.

An look ow people a look pon im,
Mi shame fi im yuh see,
Mi couldn' show mi face agen
Ef dat likkle bwoy was mi.

Eh eh, but look noh, Mama,
One nedda one a cry,
An de gal who a come out deh now
Wata full up har yeye.

But faba someting really wrong
Else dem wouldn' frighten soh,
Mama, guess wha happen,
Mi toothache gone, yuh know.

De nurse a call wi, mama,
But a couldn' fi mi time a'ready?
'Ladies before gentlemen'
Mek da gal yah go before mi.

She go a'ready? A mi one lef?
Nurse, tell de dentist noh fe badda,
Mi toothache gone fi good now.
Unless im wan' fe see mi madda?

80

Mama, yuh wouldn' force mi,
An know ow mi fraid a needle to?
No badda cyah mi een deh
Waia! Smaddy come help mi do!

Waia! Murder! Help! Police!
No mek im touch mi oh!
Mi heart no too good, doctor,
Mi wi dead from fright yuh know.

Wait, Mama, yuh hear dat?
Im cyan do nutten when mi gum swell soh,
So mi mus tek some aspirin tonight
An come back come see im tomorrow.

Die dentis is a nice man,
Im smile so sweet an warm
Wha mek dem pickney cry, cry soh?
Im wouldn' do dem no harm.

Watch dat dey one still a bawl
De pickney no hab no shame
Mi woulda nebba mek so much nize.
(Mi glad mi get whey teday all de same.)

Valerie Bloom

81

The Eyes Have it

If you can't see a
thing without a light
If you can't read this
This rhyme exactly
right If you bump
into lamp-posts in
the street Or fail to
recognize the friends
you meet If you trip
over every letter-box
Or go to school
wearing unmatching
sox If you walk
under every
bus that passes
You need

glasses

Susan Stranks

Just close your eyes...

In a minute
in my head
an empty box
a haircut
my friend's breath
a teacher's voice
a blackbird singing
what did I do on Saturday?
what shall I do at three?
a shiny floor
a squeaking chair
what does a poet eat for tea?
has a minute gone?
what can I write?
who's watching me?
this minute
in my head.

Judith Nicholls

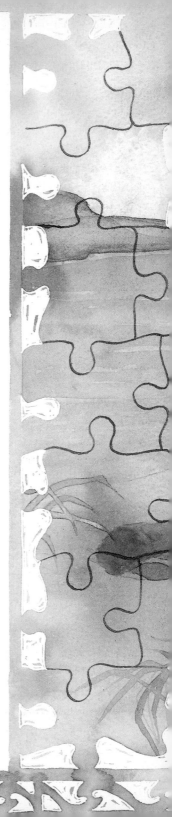

Mark's Fingers

I like my fingers.
They grip a ball,
Turn a page,
Break a fall,
Help whistle
A call.
Shake hands
And shoot
Rubber bands.
When candy is offered
They take enough.
They fill my pockets
With wonderful stuff,
And they always tell me
Smooth from rough.
They follow rivers
On a map,
They double over
When I rap,
They smack together
When I clap.
They button buttons,
Tie shoelaces,
Open doors to
Brand-new places.
They shape and float
My paper ships,
Fasten paper to
Paper clips,
And carry ice cream
To my lips...

Mary O'Neill

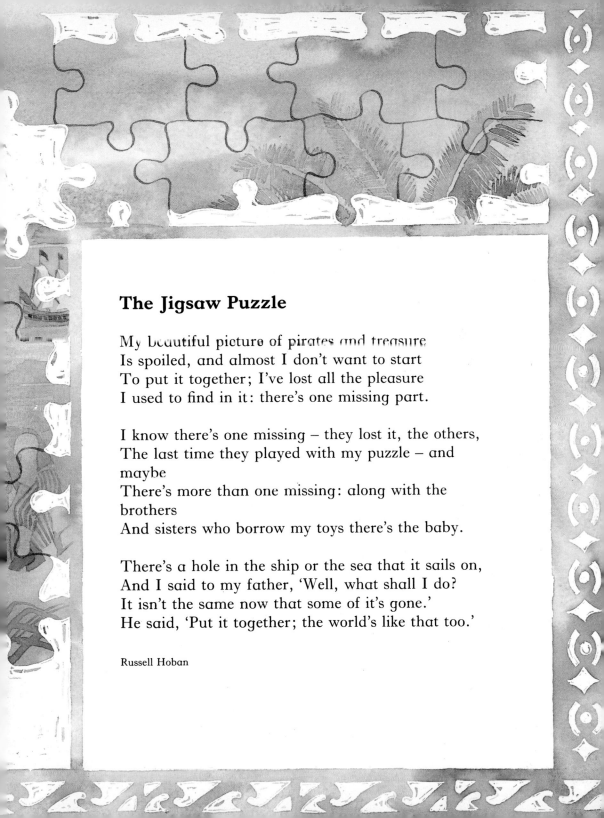

The Jigsaw Puzzle

My beautiful picture of pirates and treasure
Is spoiled, and almost I don't want to start
To put it together; I've lost all the pleasure
I used to find in it: there's one missing part.

I know there's one missing – they lost it, the others,
The last time they played with my puzzle – and
maybe
There's more than one missing: along with the
brothers
And sisters who borrow my toys there's the baby.

There's a hole in the ship or the sea that it sails on,
And I said to my father, 'Well, what shall I do?
It isn't the same now that some of it's gone.'
He said, 'Put it together; the world's like that too.'

Russell Hoban

Deaf to The World

When Dad reads the paper
Nothing will move him
He sits like a rock in his chair.
Though we shout in his ear
He just doesn't hear,
If the roof fell in
I don't think he'd care.

We can tell him a tidal wave's coming,
We can say that the sky's turned red.
He might say 'Mm – that's nice,'
But he's not heard a word that we've said.

And then, when we've given up
And we're absorbed in playing,
He'll fold the paper and interrupt us
With –
'Now what was that you were saying?'

We'll say 'It doesn't matter Dad.
It was nothing – just let us be.'
And he'll grumble and sigh to Mum,
'No one in this house
Ever talks to me!'

Then he turns the TV on,
Our Dad mutton jeff in a dream,
Watching old news
He's deaf to the world in our house
And only talks to the screen.

'Dad I've had a tooth out.'
'Dad there's a hole in my shoe.
It's not in the paper or on TV –
But we have news for you too.'

Julie Holder

Grandad's Birthday Treat

It was me Grandad's birthday
we thought it a treat
to take him to restaurant for something to eat

We found this posh steakhouse
Grandad ordered a steak
a well done chewy-chunky beefcake
(I for one thought it was a dreadful mistake)

And no sooner he began to eat his meat
out jumped his false teeth
landing clean at his feet

Me mum gave me Grandad a family glare
'Grandad didn't I tell ye to have it
soft 'n' rare?'
Grandad didn't turn the tiniest hair

He simply bent down and picked up his teeth
in no time again he was eating his meat
'What a feat,' he murmured quietly to his beard
'What a feat, Lord, bless the courage of my false teeth.'

Grace Nichols

Grizzly Bear

Rattle click, and rattle click,
My Grandpa's on the stairs;
He's breathing hard behind the door
And playing grizzly bears.

I hold my breath prepared to snatch
My Rupert from his clutch;
My rabbit sees the lifted latch
And hides inside his hutch.

And suddenly my Grandpa Bear
Explodes with swinging paws
And sweeps me up against his fur
With gently curving claws.

His muzzle snorts inside my ear,
His hot breath burns my hair,
And Grandma screams, 'Behave yourself,
And get back to your lair!'

She drives the beast back up the stairs
And slams the door in place.

Slowly,
It opens   ...
In the gap –
A stripe of Grandpa's face.

Gregory Harrison

89

Aunt Sponge and Aunt Spiker

'I look and smell,' Aunt Sponge declared, 'as
    lovely as a rose!
Just feast your eyes upon my face, observe my
    shapely nose!
Behold my heavenly silky locks!
And if I take off both my socks
You'll see my dainty toes.'
'But don't forget,' Aunt Spiker cried, 'how much
    your tummy shows!'

Aunt Sponge went red. Aunt Spiker said, 'My
    sweet, you cannot win,
Behold MY gorgeous curvy shape, my teeth, my
    charming grin!
Oh, beauteous me! How I adore
My radiant looks! And please ignore
The pimple on my chin.'
'My dear old trout!' Aunt Sponge cried out. 'You're
    only bones and skin!'

'Such loveliness as I possess can only truly shine
In Hollywood!' Aunt Sponge declared. 'Oh,
    wouldn't that be fine!
I'd capture all the nations' hearts!
They'd give me all the leading parts!
The stars would all resign!'
'I think you'd make,' Aunt Spiker said, 'a lovely
    Frankenstein.'

Roald Dahl

My Cousin Melda

My Cousin Melda
she don't make fun
she ain't afraid of anyone
even mosquitoes
when they bite her
she does bite them back
and say
'Now tell me – HOW YOU LIKE THAT?'

Grace Nichols

The Incredible Henry McHugh

I am the Incredible Henry McHugh
you should see the things that I can do!
(and I'm only two)
I can...
tie laces in knots
spit peas into pots
squirt all the cream
and scream and SCREAM!

I can...
leave toys on the stair
pour honey in hair
scatter fried rice
play football with mice
sit down on the cat
be sick in a hat
slam the door, flood the floor,
and shout 'more, MORE, MORE!'

I can telephone Timbuctoo –
and frequently do,
hurl mud pies and rocks
put jelly in socks
pull Dracula faces
and stick Mum's pins in unlikely places.

I can...
pinch, poke, tickle and stroke,
wriggle, giggle, rattle and prattle,
scrawl on the wall
spill paint down the hall
pick heads off the flowers
dribble for hours
and when things go wrong
I just sing my song.

I'M not to blame.
You know my name,
I am Henry McHugh
the INCREDIBLE!
(I'm only two).

Robert Fisher

93

Julius Sneezer

Julius Caesar was a terrible sneezer,
Or so the story goes.
When out in the forum
He'd show no decorum
By sniffing and blowing his nose.

The strength of his sneezes
Would buckle his kneeses
And drive everybody demented.
It made him anaemic and most unhygenic
'Cause hankies had not been invented.

Ian Larmont

Forth went the thunder-god

Forth went the thunder-god
Riding on his filly.
'I'm Thor,' he cried.
His horse replied:
'You forgot your thaddle, thilly.'

Anon.

There was an old man and his daughter

There was an old man and his daughter
Who fell head over heels in deep water.
  Said the man, 'Her can't swim,'
  (And no more couldn't him)
'I wish someone had tortoise, or taughter.'

Anon.

Insides

I'm very grateful to my skin
For keeping all my insides in –
I do so hate to think about
What I would look like inside-out.

Colin West

A Cow's Outside

A cow's outside is mainly hide,
undoubtedly this leather
retains a cow's insides inside,
and holds a cow together.

Jack Prelutsky

'Are you sitting comfortably?'

Newscaster:
  'Victor
  (a boa constrictor)
   's escaped down a loo.
   He's still missing
  and may surface for air,
slithering, hissing,
anywhere
  coming
    up through
      the plumbing.
        Don't linger long
     whatever you do,
  It's hard
    to restrict a
      slide-away
       snake –
    it may swim up
         the U
      bend,
     surprising
  the user –
    not me,
     I hope,
       but . . .
          you?'

Ian Serraillier

I Have a Hippopotamus

I have a hippopotamus
I keep it in the bath
it is a happy hippo
but every time it laughs
water floods across the floor
and mum goes on the warpath

She tells me – keeping hippos
in a house is daft
they should be on the telly
or in a photograph
why can't you keep something sensible
like a lion or giraffe?

Dave Calder

A young man from Berwick-on-Tweed

A young man from Berwick-on-Tweed
Kept a very strange thing on a lead.
He was never once seen
To give it a clean
Or anything else it might need.

Michael Palin

Accidentally

Once – I didn't mean to,
but that
was that –
I yawned in the sunshine
and swallowed a gnat.

I'd rather eat mushrooms
and bullfrogs' legs,
I'd rather have pepper
all over my eggs

than open my mouth
on a sleepy day
and close on a gnat
going down that way.

It tasted sort of salty.
It didn't hurt a bit.
I accidentally ate a gnat
and that
was
it!

Maxine W. Kumin

98

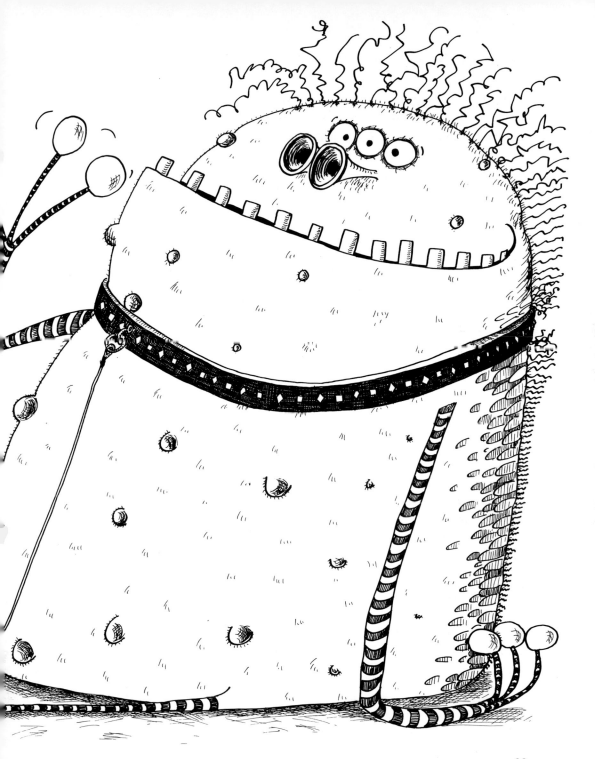

My Dog

My dog belongs to no known breed,
A bit of this and that.
His head looks like a small haystack
He's lazy, smelly, fat.

If I say, 'Sit!', he walks away.
When I throw stick or ball
He flops down in the grass as if
He had no legs at all,

And looks at me with eyes that say,
'You threw the thing, not me.
You want it back, then get it back.
Fair's fair, you must agree.'

He is a thief. Last week but one
He stole the Sunday Roast
And showed no guilt at all as we
Sat down to beans on toast.

The only time I saw him run –
And he went like a flash –
Was when a mugger in the park
Tried to steal my cash.

My loyal brave companion flew
Like a missile to the gate
And didn't stop till safely home.
He left me to my fate.

And would I swap him for a dog
Obedient, clean and good,
An honest, faithful, lively chap?
Oh boy, I would! I would!

Vernon Scannell

101

Letting in the light

I am warm wrapped in my fur
My wobbly legs resting as I lie here,
My eyes still closed.
Soon they will open
Letting in the light,
And when I see
I'll spin the world round in tumbles
As I play chasing my tail,
Or hunt specks of dust in the sunlight
And wash the paws I have never seen.
My mother washes my face
Her tongue smoothing my fur,
I hear her purr,
And see, yes, see some pink.
Her busy tongue, her whiskers,
Fur and eyes so orange bright,
She bends towards me,
Licking and licking,
And over I go.
I see light everywhere
And begin to know
I have opened my eyes.

Elizabeth Lindsay

At the Zoo

Tiger
eyes dark with
half-remembered forest night,
stalks an empty cage.

Wolf
still on his lone rock
stares at the uncaged stars and
cries into the night.

Judith Nicholls

Tiger

Terrifyingly fierce
I glow through my stripes as I
Gracefully prowl at
Evening and night.
Regard and admire me.

John Cotton

Sloth

Sleepy, sleepy,
Looking out of my big round eyes,
Oh I wish I could sleep high in the trees
Through night and through day
Happily dreaming.

John Cotton

Hannah said

Hannah said:
Did you know
Elephants have three sets of teeth?
And when the third set falls out
They die.
They cannot eat
Because they can no longer chew
Their food.

Sandra sucked her lip,
Then gently probed
Her loose tooth
With her tongue.
I'm glad I'm not an elephant,
She thought.

Hannah said:
Did you know
That in America
There is an owl
Which behaves like a snake?

When it is cornered,
The burrowing owl
Hisses like an angry rattlesnake
To scare away the squirrels
Whose home it has stolen.

Sandra pretended to be interested
Then, when Hannah turned her back,
She stuck out her tongue.
So what? Who cares?
She hissed.

John Foster

Fox

Sun plushed eve
and mauve the chilly air
Ice brittle grass squeaks
and creaks as the lone
fox
trips his slinky way
along the inky hedge
He barks and splits the misty air with his
gasping yell.

Laurence Smith

First Fox

A big fox stands in the spring grass,
Glossy in the sun, chestnut bright,
Plumb centre of the open meadow, a leaf
From a picturebook.

Forepaws delicately nervous,
Thick brush on the grass
He rakes the air for the scent
Of the train rushing by.

My first fox,
Wiped from my eye,
In a moment of train-time.

Pamela Gillilan

Firefox

Fox fox
coat of fire
bush of flame
setting light
to April woods
firework trail
of powder, fuse
that sets aglow
with green and gold
the willow wands
the meadow grass
the pasture ponds
the primrose banks.

Fox fox fox
from winter runs
with torch for tail
and touches spring
to hill and copse
his foxfire fingers
flaming hedges
spreading shoots of
shivering blossom
in the sun – the ghost
of summertime
that trots beside
his crimson shadow's
violet and bluebell glades –

mysterious barks – fox, fox,
fox, fox-fox, fox, fox-fox-fox!

James Kirkup

109

Tortoise and Hare

(or: Slow, Slow, Quick, Quick, Slow ....)

Slowly the tortoise raised her head,
stared slowly at the hare;
slowly stepped towards the line
and waited there.

Calmly she heard the starting gun,
crawled calmly down the track;
calmly watched the hare race on
and not look back.

Quickly the hare ran out of sight,
chased quickly through the wood;
quickly fled through fern and moss,
through leaf and mud.

Swiftly he leapt past hedge and field,
sped swiftly for his prize;
briefly stopped to take a rest –
and closed his eyes.

Slowly the tortoise reached the wood,
slowly she ambled on.
The hare raced proudly through his dreams;
the tortoise won.

Judith Nicholls

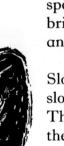

The Lion and the Echo

The King of the Beasts, deep in the wood,
Roared as loudly as it could.
Right away the echo came back
And the lion thought itself under attack.

'What voice is it that roars like mine?'
The echo replied 'Mine, mine.'

'Who might you be?' asked the furious lion,
'I'm king of this jungle, this jungle is mine.'
And the echo came back a second time,
'This jungle is mine, is mine, is mine.'

The lion swore revenge if only it could
Discover the intruder in the wood.
It roared 'Coward! Come out and show yourself!'
But the fearless echo replied simply '...elf.'

'Come out,' roared the lion, 'Enough deceit,
Do you fear for your own defeat?'
But all the echo did was repeat
'Defeat...defeat...'

Frightened by every conceivable sound,
The exhausted lion sank to the ground.
A bird in a tree looked down and it said,
'Dear lion, I'm afraid that what you hear
Is simply the voice of your lion-sized fear.'

Brian Patten

Minotaur

in the middle of the sea lies an island
in the middle of the island stands a palace
in the middle of the palace is a maze
of darkened rooms and alleyways
endless walls and hidden doors
miles and miles of corridors
here shadows fall and footsteps sound
echoing along the ground
here is my home
I am minotaur
half-man half-bull
shaggy-headed golden horns
hear me bellow hear my roar
see the slavering of my jaw
round the corner here I wait
flaring nostrils sniff the air
for here or somewhere a door may open
and I will enter
your dream
of the sea
and in the middle of the sea lies an island
in the middle of the island stands a palace
in the middle of the palace is a maze
of darkened rooms and alleyways
endless walls and hidden doors
miles and miles of corridors
here shadows fall and footsteps sound
echoing along the ground
here is my home
I am ... waiting

Robert Fisher

114

Alien

On his own planet, Alien was handsome
but here his shape would have been
unbelievable – except
that it was magically shielded.

When an elephant met him
he saw a trunk;
when a giraffe met him
he saw a long neck;
a rabbit saw twitching whiskers
and furry ears. To us his face
seemed ordinary, though his eyes
could change to the seven colours of light.
And why did his grey cloak
reach
right
down
to
the
ground
?

Pamela Gillilan

117

The Tower

The squat; black tower
Silhouetted stark against an orange sky
Stands sinister and high
Above the circling copse
Of polished beech.

It is not haunted;
No-one has ever suggested it.

There are no creaking doors,
No footsteps pacing upper floors,
No shadowy stairs with shapes,
No sudden chills,
No curtains falling into place,
No face,
No misty outline passing through a wall,
No spectral presences at all.

And nobody has ever heard
A clank of chains
Or wolfish howl,
Or seen a monk in robe and cowl
Full in the moon's cold orb
Casting no shadow.

I thought I saw a light
From the turret room
One night,
But it was early, only nine
So I sat undecided
On the spiral stairs
For half an hour.

Then, no other way to the top,
I climbed,
Pushed at the panelled door ...
The room, the sole high narrow room
Lit by my lamp
Was empty,
The window closed and cobwebbed,
The table bare
Except for a smoking candle,
The wick still warm
In its pool of glassy wax.

Gregory Harrison

The World the First Time

What is that howling, my mother
Howling out of the sky;
What is it rustles the branches and leaves
And throws the cold snow in my eye?

That is the wind, my wolf son,
The breath of the world passing by,
That flattens the grasses and whips up the lake
And hurls clouds and birds through the sky.

What is that eye gleaming red, mother
Gleaming red in the face of the sky;
Why does it stare at me so mother
Why does its fire burn my eye?

That is the sun, my wolf child,
That changes dark night into day,
That warms your fur and the pine-needled floor
And melts the cold snows away.

And who is this serpent that glides, mother,
And winds the dark rocks among,
And laughs and sings as he glides through my paws
And feels so cool on my tongue?

That is the river, my curious son,
That no creature alive can outrun
He cuts out the valleys and watery lakes
And was here when the world first begun.

And whose is that face that I see, mother,
That face in the water so clear,
Why when I try to catch him
Does he suddenly disappear?

He is closer to you than your brother,
Closer than your father or me,
He'll run beside you your long life through,
For it is yourself – that you see.

Gareth Owen

Have you ever thought?

A comb has teeth but can't bite,
A shoe has a tongue but can't talk,
Rulers have feet and tables have legs
Yet neither of them can walk.

A chair has an arm but no elbow,
A clock has two hands but can't hold,
Hills have brows, and corn has ears
Though they never turn blue in the cold.

Needles and spuds have eyes
But not one of them can see,
And though a jug has a lip, and a tunnel a mouth,
They can't drink coffee or tea.

Rocks and clocks have faces,
Books have backs and a spine,
A well's got a bottom, a sausage a skin;
There's a neck on a bottle of wine.

Roads have hard shoulders but can't shrug,
A car has a body plus parts,
Tools have chests and chimneys have breasts.
But only people – and lettuce – have hearts!

Jacqueline Brown

SPUDS

ONLY PEOPLE
- AND LETTUCE
- HAVE HEARTS!

LETTUCE BE TOGETHER

Questions

Why is the rocking-chair rocking?
  Why does it rock in the windless air
of the sunny veranda – Why
  does it rock when there's no one there?

Why is the swing door swinging?
  Why does it swing at the foot of the stair?
Why, like the chair, does it keep on moving
  back and forth, when there's no one there?

Why is the doorbell ringing? Why
  does it ring through the empty flat
when there's nobody pressing the button
  and nobody stands on the welcome mat?

Something has happened here. What can it be?
  Why have they all gone away like this?
Why are the windows all open? And why
  does that record keep turning, hiss upon hiss...?

James Kirkup

Index of first lines

Acknowledgements

The following poems are appearing for the first time in this collection and are printed by permission of the author unless otherwise stated.
Moira Andrew: *Count me out*, © 1987 Moira Andrew. Leo Aylen: *Kitchen Adventure*, © 1987 Leo Aylen. Valerie Bloom: *Chicken Dinner*; *Visit to de Dentist*, both © 1987 Valerie Bloom. Jacqueline Brown: *Wellie Weather*; *Have you ever thought?*, both © 1987 Jacqueline Brown. Dave Calder: *I Have a Hippopotamus*, © 1987 Dave Calder. Stanley Cook: *Mouthful*; *The Tunnel*, both © 1987 Stanley Cook. Wendy Cope: *Huff*, © 1987 Wendy Cope. Pie Corbett: *Take Two*, © 1987 Pie Corbett. John Cotton: *Tiger*; *Sloth*, both © 1987 John Cotton. John Cunliffe: *The Wind in a Tree*, © 1987 John Cunliffe. Peter Dixon: *Infant School Disaster*, © 1987 Peter Dixon. Berlie Doherty: *Hob-goblin*, © 1987 Berlie Doherty. Eric Finney: *Do You Mind?*; *Don't Panic*, both © 1987 Eric Finney. Robert Fisher: *The Tree in Season*; *Minotaur*; *The Incredible Henry McHugh*, all © 1987 Robert Fisher. Frank Flynn: *Floating a Plate*, © 1987 Frank Flynn. John Foster: *Month by Month*; *Early to Bed*; *Hannah said*, all © 1987 John Foster. Pamela Gillilan: *Fox*; *Alien*, both © 1987 Pamela Gillilan. Gregory Harrison: *The Lighthouse*; *Grizzly bear*; *The Tower*, all © 1987 Gregory Harrison. Julie Holder: *Playground Count*; *Change of Mind*; *Wet Winter Evening*; *The Storm*; *Deaf to the World*, all © 1987 Julie Holder. James Kirkup: *Our Goalie*; *My Sledge*; *Thunder in the Mountains*; *The Sand Castle*; *Firefox*; *Questions*, all © James Kirkup 1987. John Kitching: *Change*; *Weak Week*; *Beware*, all © 1987 John Kitching. Ian Larmont: *Julius Sneezer*, © 1987 Ian Larmont. Wes Magee: *Windows*, © 1987 Wes Magee. Grace Nichols: *I like to stay up*; *Grandad's birthday treat*, *My cousin Melda* all © 1987 Grace Nichols. Judith Nicholls: *Winter*; *Timeless*; *Midnight Forest*; *Grudges*; *Just close your eyes...*, *At the Zoo: Tiger, Wolf*; *Tortoise and Hare*, all © 1987 Judith Nicholls. Gareth Owen: *The World the First Time*, © 1987 Gareth Owen. Joan Poulson: *School break*, © 1987 Joan Poulson. Vernon Scannell: My *Dog*, © 1987 Vernon Scannell. Ian Serraillier: *Are you sitting comfortably?*, © 1987 Ian Serraillier. Sheila Simmons: *After Dark*, © 1987 Sheila Simmons. Colin West: *Knitting*; *Insides*, both © 1987 Colin West.

The cover is by Chris Swee, and photographed by Tessa Wilkinson.

The illustrations are by Judy Brown, Linda Farquharson, Gary Goodman, Sue Green, Norman Johnson, Sian Leetham, Julia Rowntree, Gill Scriven, Dulce Tobin, John Watson.

The publishers would like to thank Oxford Scientific Films Picture Library for permission to reproduce the photograph on p.104/105.

We are grateful for permission to include the following previously published material in this anthology:

John Agard: 'Who the Cap Fit Let Them Wear it' from *Say It Again, Granny* by John Agard, illustrated by Susanna Gretz. Reprinted by permission of The Bodley Head.   Margaret Wise Brown: 'The Secret Song' from *Nibble Nibble*. Text copyright © 1959 by William Scott, Inc. Reprinted by permission of Harper & Row, Publishers, Inc.   Stanley Cook: 'Tunnel' from *Meet and Write* edited by Alan and Sandy Brownjohn. Reprinted by permission of the author.   Katherine Craig: 'The Useful Art of Knitting', © Katherine Craig, reprinted from *All Sorts of Poems*, ed. Ann Thwaite, Angus & Robertson (UK) Ltd.   Roald Dahl: 'Aunt Sponge and Aunt Spiker' from *James and the Giant Peach* (Allen & Unwin/ Penguin Books). Copyright © 1961 by Roald Dahl. Reprinted by permission of Murray Pollinger, Literary Agent, and the American Publisher, Alfred A Knopf Inc.   Dennis Doyle: 'Shirley Said', first published in *Apricot Rhymes* (Commonplace Workshop) and reprinted in *I Like That Stuff*, ed. Morag Styles (Cambridge University Press).   Gwen Dunn: 'I Went Back' from *The Beaver Book of School Verse*, ed. Jennifer Curry. Reprinted by permission of the author. Richard Edwards: 'Our Pond' and 'Snow' from *The Word Party*. Reprinted by permission of John Johnson (Authors' Agent) Ltd., and Lutterworth Press.   Eric Finney: 'Don't Panic' from *Billy and Me and the Igloo and Other Poems*. Reprinted by permission of the author, and Edward Arnold (Publ.) Ltd.   Robert Fisher: 'Minotaur' from *Amazing Monsters* ed. Robert Fisher (Faber & Faber 1982); 'The Incredible Henry McHugh' from *Funny Folk*, ed. Robert Fisher (Faber & Faber 1986). Reprinted by permission of the author.   Russell Hoban: 'The Jigsaw Puzzle' from *Allsorts 3*, ed. Ann Thwaite. Reprinted by permission of David Higham Associates Ltd.   Maxine Kumin: 'Accidentally', from *No One Writes a Letter to a Snail*. Text copyright © 1962 by Maxine W Kumin. Reprinted by permission of Curtis Brown Ltd. Elizabeth Lindsay: 'Letting in the Light', © Elizabeth Lindsay, published in *Stories and Rhymes* (BBC Publications, 1981).   Doug Macleod: 'Vampire Visit' from *In the Garden of Bad Things*. Reprinted by permission of Penguin Books Australia Ltd.   Marc Matthews: 'I Love the Friday Night Smells of Mammie Baking' from *I Like That Stuff*, ed. Morag Styles. Reprinted by permission of Cambridge University Press.   Roger McGough: 'Storm' from *After the Merrymaking*. Reprinted by permission of Jonathan Cape Ltd., and A. D. Peters Ltd.   Lilian Moore: 'Snowy Morning' from *I Thought I heard the City*. Copyright © 1969 by Lilian Moore. Reprinted by permission of Marian Reiner for the author.   Bonnie Nims: 'How to Get There' from *I Wish I Lived at the Playground* (1972). Reprinted by permission of the author.   Leslie